M000295300

The 7 Step Transition from Student to Professional

LATOYA PEARSON

Published by Latoya Pearson, LLC

Cover design by Vashti Fowler
Back cover photo by Justin L. Rigdon
Creative Direction by Latoya Pearson and Tamiko Lowry
Pugh, Author/Writer Services

Printed in the United States of America

ISBN-13: 978-0692927908
ISBN-10: 0692927905

DEDICATION

This 7 Step Transition from Student to Professional is dedicated to every student that attended my workshop, heard the information during a classroom presentation or spoke with me at an event over the past few years. Working with each of you and witnessing your success, has truly inspired me to continue sharing this information. I am greatly appreciative of your trust in the process and above all, your hard work. You were dedicated and determined to improve your interviewing skills and land the job you were seeking. You carved time out of your schedule to practice and sharpen your knife. Whether it was via phone, voice memos or FaceTime – you found the time to role-play and understand your vulnerable points. I know I made you uncomfortable and put you on the spot, but all of you persevered and thanked me later. I knew you could do it which is why I continued to push you. I am grateful to all of you for allowing me the opportunity to work with you and help you build your interviewing muscle. As you prosper and flourish into your careers, don't forget I'm still just an email, phone call or text message away. Stay focused and go after your dreams! Thank you!

ACKNOWLEDGEMENTS

To my mother: There are no words that would ever articulate your true impact on my life. You defeated insurmountable challenges to pave a path to success. Your optimism is contagious, and your genuineness is unmeasurable. I love you dearly.

To my college professor, Dr. Gail Thompkins: From the day I left your classroom until now, I've always said that your class saved my life. Professional Development I and II were filled with tons of life lessons. You taught me so much about myself and how to use my skills to be successful. Over the past few years, you have become a mentor, spiritual advisor, and a life coach. I'm forever grateful for your contribution to my life and the experiences I've gained from your knowledge and wisdom.

To my mentor, Norris Wright: My workshops grew legs after we brainstormed for hours about the "true" interview process and the formula for a successful transition. Thank you for your dedication and persistence in helping me with this project and many others.

To my publisher, Tamiko Lowry-Pugh, LLC: You are truly an amazing person, and I am privileged to have had the opportunity to work with you. This book was just a workshop without you. Thank you for your guidance, industry knowledge and coaching to get me to the finish line.

CONTENTS

INTRODUCTION

This is the most exciting time of your life. You are finishing the college years and entering into your young adult years. You have grown from a teenager into a young adult in a short period of time. Think about everything that you have accomplished while in school. The long days and all-nighters you pulled to meet a deadline. The numerous projects and papers that stretched your boundaries and enhanced your knowledge. All the people you have met and all the new relationships and friendships that you've established. You will never experience anything like this again.

So, let me ask you a few questions.

- Do you have it all figured out?
- Are you ready to tackle the world and make an impact?
- Do you know exactly what you'll be doing post-graduation?
- Have you selected a career or have an idea of what you want to pursue?
- Have you mastered your interviewing techniques?

- Have you figured out the key components of interview preparation?

If you answered "no" to any of those questions, you're not alone. Over 50% of Junior and Senior students are in the same boat. Many have a good idea of what they want to do but have no idea of how to actually get there. That's what I call "the transition." It's the time between your last year of school and your first year on the job. There are ways to start preparing for the transition during your first or second year, so by the start of Senior year; you'll be ready to go. Most students wait until their second semester of Junior year or first semester of Senior year to start preparing for their transition. There's never any harm in starting early because by the time you become a Senior not only are you very prepared for the transition, but you're also very secure in your career selection and post-graduate decisions.

Why is the transition important? You may be thinking; it can't be that hard to get into the company or field of my choice. If those are your thoughts, I hate to break the news to you, but it's actually more challenging now than it's ever been in the past. According to a Reuters.com article by Elvina Nawagan, "recent college graduates in the United States face a more challenging job market, causing them to remain unemployed or take lower paying jobs than their counterparts in the past two decades. While it generally takes new graduates some time to transition into the job market, today's graduates are having an even tougher time." Generation Y is the largest population of all generations. The number of graduates seeking employment is the first hurdle, but companies are excited to welcome this generation into the workforce. "Millennials are being sought after for their creative, fresh approach, drive and ambition as well as their passion to learn new things and improve efficiencies," said a seasoned Human Resources Professional. This is the reason why the transition is important and essential to your success. Although the market may seem tough, the opportunities are there.

This book will guide you down the path of transitioning or connecting your passion with your talent in order to select the perfect career. It will also help in developing your interviewing skills to secure the job as well as provide helpful tips to being successful within the first 365 days. The seven steps will help you answer the following questions:

- What is my passion?
- What are my key talents and skills?
- What's the difference between a job and a career?
- How do I secure a Shadow Day?
- What specific things should I look for when researching a company or industry?
- How do I create a captivating resume to secure an interview?
- What are the key components of an interview?
- How do I prepare for an interview?
- What can I do to ensure a great start on the new job?

The goal is to help college students transition into the workplace but not just an everyday 8-5 job; an actual career. I've spent many years training and developing students and even professionals. Throughout this time, I realized there are a lot of people who do not understand what it takes to get in the corporate world. It's only easy for the people who are privileged enough to know someone or are related to someone already on the other side. The rest of us are on our own.

According to a Washington Post article by Susan Svrluga, more than 4 out of 5 students graduate without a job. Does that sound outrageous? How are students going to school for 4-5 years and leaving without a job? The purpose of getting a higher education is to better position yourself for a successful career. So, why are so many students graduating without a job?

About a year ago, I was on a college campus during the last month of the spring semester. I began to randomly ask graduating seniors "have you confirmed plans for post-graduation?" I used those specific words because I knew some students were headed to graduate school. After asking 45 students, here were the results:

- 9 – Received job offer & accepted.
- 11 – Still interviewing (no job offers yet)
- 8 – No interviews scheduled but wants a corporate career.
- 6 – Accepted into graduate school.
- 11 – Completely undecided.

In that short time on campus, I realized how unprepared many of the students were for their transition. After I asked the question, some gave me a blank stare look as if I was asking them to solve a scientific equation. I gave each of them my email and phone number and told them to call me if they wanted me to help them with the transition. Unfortunately, they were graduating in less than a month, so it may take up to 6 months or so post-graduation to find the perfect career, but I was willing to go through the process with them.

In the Fall of 2008, I volunteered to help out with the recruiting process in Atlanta. As an organization, we were predominantly looking for students with extensive leadership skills and a passion for sales. As I went through the interviews, I noticed a gap. For the record, I interviewed students who had very impressive resumes and a wealth of experience relative to the average college student. Some studied abroad while others had four or five internships or just simply held down a regular job. They all had valuable resumes, but most of them were not very comfortable with talking about their experience within the interview environment. It was not an issue of lack of content but more of a delivery gap.

I remember interviewing Dennis Lee. He was a graduating senior majoring in Business. Dennis completed two internships with Coca-Cola and Rubbermaid which both guided him down the path of sales. He was extremely compassionate with excellent interpersonal skills. I was very impressed after speaking to him during our Information Session which is held the evening before the interviews. Dennis knew a lot about the organization and asked great questions related to the Sales Development program. I was definitely looking forward to interviewing him the next day. He was the second candidate on my interview schedule and arrived 30 minutes before his interview time slot. Again, I was impressed. I called him back to the interview room, and we immediately started the small talk. I noticed people used small talk to calm their nerves but I typically use it to assess the mood of the interviewer, and that is exactly what Dennis was doing. I could tell he wasn't nervous but more so trying to figure out "Latoya, the interviewer" versus the person from last night.

We started the interview with a few self-reflective questions, and I could tell Dennis was comfortable, but he was too comfortable. He was slouching in his chair and used very casual language when answering the questions. This was my first disappointing moment. As the interview entered the behavioral based question phase, Dennis struggled to deliver his examples in the interview format. I could tell he knew what he was talking about but his examples didn't flow and he gave irrelevant details that prolonged his interview. He did not write down a single question which came back to bite him when he drifted off track. I was tremendously disappointed by this point. I had such high hopes for Dennis because he had the leadership skills and sales passion that were both perfectly fitting for our program. Unfortunately, his delivery killed his chance to advance to the next round of interviews.

I continued to see this year after year. It was very disappointing, and I felt there was nothing that I could do because, by the time I saw them, it was too late. In 2014, I got with my recruiting co-lead, and we brainstormed on how we could help the students. We talked to professors, faculty, career services, deans and the students as well. We wanted to give them useful interviewing tips before the interview, so they understood the process and had time to practice. That was essentially our gap. We always gave them the information the night before the interview which gave them no time to truly practice. At that time, we started giving interview workshops during classroom time which was extremely beneficial to all students. The goal was to educate students on the interviewing process no matter which company they choose for employment. The workshops grew each year on that campus, and I had the opportunity to conduct the workshop for other schools in the Atlanta and Charlotte areas.

I remember having lunch with two friends at a local restaurant, where we talked about our personal and professional goals. I love those outings because we get a chance to challenge each other and talk through solutions. I told the girls I wanted to find a way to get the workshop content out to more people without having to travel from campus to campus. We discussed several ideas, and that became my homework.

About 3 months later, I was in Washington D.C. attending a Leadership Retreat for the National Coalition of 100 Black Women. I met Tamiko Lowry-Pugh from the Atlanta area after the first day. We were sitting in the bar area having a bite to eat. The conversation shifted to the topic of passions and sharing our personal experiences. I shared my passion for helping people develop professionally and the workshops I'd conducted over the years. She immediately said, "You should put your workshop content into a book." I remember looking a little perplexed because I never thought about writing a book. Tamiko asked me to explain the workshop to her and as I started to explain she said "Ok. That's chapter one. What's the next topic?" I was stunned. She broke the entire workshop down into chapters as we sat in the bar area of the Westin Hotel. I was more than impressed, and I knew I had to do it.

After a few years of sharing in classrooms or during evening receptions, I am now sharing this workshop with all of you. So, get ready to take notes and challenge yourself. This is for your personal development, and it's filled with many tips and ideas to help you tackle the transition into the professional world. Are you ready?

STEP ONE
The Assessment

Thinking back to my junior year at Florida A&M University, I can vividly recall sitting in my townhouse thinking about my future and what life would be like after I left Tallahassee, Florida. I was anxious, curious and a little scared of what was ahead for me in less than a year. Had I chosen the right major? Did I optimize my internships enough? So many thoughts and emotions were going through my head. I was three semesters away from graduating yet a lifetime away from really knowing what I wanted to do. Many of my friends had it all figured out. They knew exactly what they wanted to do. While speaking with them, I found myself feeling less than successful and thinking "how did I get this far and still feeling lost about my future?" Then it hit me – well sort of. Over the next two weeks, something big happened that brought clarity to my future in a way I could have never foreseen.

It was the start of Professional Development I (PDI) with Dr. Gail Thompkins. She was the professor all the upperclassmen warned us of. Dr. Thompkins was strict with very high expectations of her students. If you were running late to her class, you might as well skip it because no one entered her class late, mainly because she locked the door after she walked in. On day one of class, students typically did not care for her direct and slightly brash demeanor. By the end of the semester, students were hanging out in her office and working hard to meet her expectations because we realized her class was much more than just a two credit hour PD class. Dr. Thompkins strived to make you better than you were the first day of class. She gave real and transparent feedback. She would push you outside of your comfort zone until you were no longer uncomfortable. Dr. Thompkins was also your mother. She was a sounding board for many and gave the best advice on conquering those young adult issues. Today, she is still a prominent figure in my life and many others.

Two weeks after pondering about my future in my townhouse, Dr. Thompkins introduced me to "The Assessment." It was a 30 question survey that would allow me to introspectively determine what I was passionate about and help me understand what I would be willing to do if money was not my focus. I remember sitting in class listening intensely as she explained the assessment and the purpose. I couldn't believe it. This was exactly what I needed. I'd never heard of an assessment, so the thought was exciting, to say the least.

What is an assessment & why is it important?

An assessment is simply an evaluation and in this case a self and career evaluation. The primary goal of completing a career assessment is to help you narrow down your career opportunities or completely decide on a specific career. Many students enter into their senior year of college without a clue of what they will be doing in less than 365 days. This typically leads to them settling for any company that will make them an offer without considering the actual job responsibilities or their personal interest level. This is why it is important to complete an assessment. The key is to find the perfect connection between your talent/skill level and your passion or interest. Your passion drives the reason why you wake up and want to go to work each morning. The skill level or talent drives your ability to complete the job every day. Both are equally important which is why you should take the time to complete an assessment to ensure you achieve a good match.

It is very important that you complete at least one assessment, but for comparison purposes, I would recommend 2-3. There are many online assessments out there, and they are all setup differently, but all of them will lead you to a list of suggested occupations. Here are a few websites that offer FREE assessments but feel free to explore other sites as well.

1.   MAPP Assessment:

www.assessment.com - This is a 71 question assessment that requires you to select a least favorite and most favorite statement out of three statements. During this assessment, be sure you read each statement and take your time selecting the most likely and least likely of the three. If you find that you like all of them, think about being in a 20-30 year career within each statement. Is that something you can do for 30 years? On the other hand, maybe that is just something you are interested in doing for 30

days. Either way, it will definitely help you narrow down the most likely statement based on those thoughts. At the end of the assessment, you will receive your results by categories: interest in job content, temperament for the job, aptitude for the job, people, things, data, reasoning, mathematical capacity and language capacity. You will also have the option to receive five top career matches either by category or by keyword search. I would suggest using the category option because you can see the entire list of categories, which could be helpful as you are trying to align your passion and skill set. Once you select the category, a list of careers for that category will appear below. Select the one that interests you most and click the "Run MAPP Match" button at the bottom. A level one or level two match is the best match for you. Once you find the career with the level one or two match, click the "Quick Career Description" and "Extensive Career Details" on the right side. Your chart should look something like this.

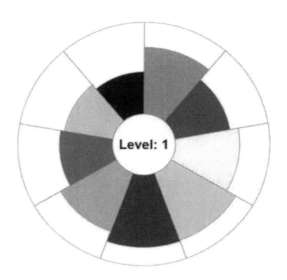

The Quick Career Description will be a short sentence describing your ideal career. The Extensive Career Details consists of pertinent information that will help you determine if this is the right career for you.

1) Education: degree, certification or license requirements

2) Advancement Potential: what is the normal career path or next level job?

3) Important Qualities: What skills are needed to be successful?

4) Duties: What are the specific job duties?

5) Work Schedule: Typical hours and/or shift expectations

6) Similar Occupations: a list of 6-8 job titles, job descriptions, entry-level education

7) requirement and median annual pay

8) Job Outlook: what is the projected growth of this job/career through 2022?

Now for a fee, you can upgrade and get access to additional information that pertains to your assessment. I would only suggest that if you feel the FREE results are not applicable and you want more information.

2. Aptitude Tests:

www.oprah.com/omagazine/Aptitude-Tests-Career-Assessment,

The Johnson O'Connor Research Foundation, put together five aptitude test to help assess your career. Download and print all five test. There are 3-5 questions or a writing/activity assignment. Next, you will find the answers to all five tests. Compare your answers to the correct answers. It is okay if you did not perform well on all five test. Look at the test that you answer all of the questions correctly and pay close attention to the career suggestions for each of those.

3. Career Quiz:

https://www.princetonreview.com/quiz/career-quiz this is a 24-question assessment that will only take a few minutes to complete. After completing the test, you will receive your results as well as recommended careers. The results are broken into color groups, and your "interest" and your "style" will both receive a color group and explanation. After reading those, move on to the recommended careers tab where you will find a list of 20-30 career choices. This site does a great job with explaining the day in the life, how to pay your dues or earn respect, the present and future of this career and the quality of life for entry-level, mid-career and tenure. Take your time as you are reviewing each career and try to narrow your list down to 10 or less.

4. Holland Code Test:

https://www.123test.com/career-test/ this is a short 15-question test where you choose a most interesting and a least interesting picture showing specific work activities. Each activity is related to a specific personality type, which is derived from Dr. John Holland's theory of career and vocational choice, known as the Holland Codes. Once you complete the test, the results are six letters representing your top matched personality type down to the last. There are six personality types in Holland's model:

- Realistic: practical, physical, concrete, hands-on, machine and tool-oriented
- Investigative: analytical, intellectual, scientific, explorative, thinker
- Artistic: creative, original, independent, chaotic, inventive, media, graphics and text
- Social: cooperative, supporting, helping, healing/nurturing, teaching
- Enterprising: competitive environments, leadership, persuading, status
- Conventional: detail-oriented, organizing, clerical

You should see a chart that will show your breakdown by percentages. After you review the percentages, look at the suggested occupations and record the top 3-5 for comparison with the other tests.

Every assessment is different and asks different questions, so be sure to take more than one and then compare all of the results. Look at the similarities first because that is probably your most dominant skill or interest. Are there any common trends that are related to the suggested occupations from your assessments? Did a specific career show up within the results of multiple assessments? Take time to digest those similarities and reflect on them. Start listing the careers that spark your interest the most, so you now have a list of potential careers that align with your skill set and passion. Then look at the suggestions that were different. Think about yourself in those environments and reflect on those feelings. You may have received one career suggestion from one assessment but not from any of the others, and that is okay. You should still consider those careers as well. Record those outcomes and your notes about each of them.

Meet Kenya. She is a Food Science major at Florida A&M University. Kenya has plans to attend Dental School upon graduation followed by a Postgraduate Orthodontics Program. After taking the 71-question MAPP assessment, Kenya selected the Healthcare Practitioner category and Orthodontist as a career. The Orthodontist career path was a level two match for Kenya, which aligns almost perfectly with her passion as well as her skills. Here is her breakdown from www.assessment.com

Category: Healthcare Practitioner & Technical
Career/Occupation: Orthodontist

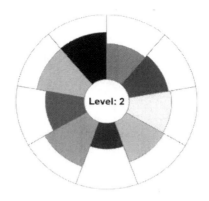

Quick Job Description for an Orthodontist: Examine, diagnose, treat dental malocclusions and oral cavity anomalies. Design and fabricate appliances to realign teeth and jaws to produce and maintain normal function and to improve appearance.

Important Qualities:
- Communication skills – must be able to communicate effectively with patients,

dental hygienists, dental assistants, and the receptionist.

- <u>Detail oriented</u> – must be detail oriented, so patients receive appropriate treatments and medications. They must also pay attention to space, shape, and the color of teeth. For example, they may need to closely match a false tooth with a patient's other teeth.
- <u>Dexterity</u> – must be good at working with their hands.
- <u>Leadership skills</u> – when working in your own practice, this skill is required to manage staff.
- <u>Organizational skills</u> – must be able to keep accurate records of patient care and services.
- <u>Patience</u> – must be able to work for long periods of time with patients who need special attention such as children or patients with a fear of dental work.
- <u>Physical stamina</u> – must be comfortable performing physical tasks such as bending over patients for an extended period of time.

- <u>Problem-solving skills</u> – must have strong problem-solving skills to evaluate the patients' symptoms and be able to choose the appropriate treatments.

Now that Kenya has taken her assessment, she can start focusing building the specified skills necessary for becoming an orthodontist.

Other Assessment Options

There are many people who are not fans of taking online assessments, and that is okay. Think about the characters on your favorite television show or movie. Have you ever thought, "That looks interesting" or, "I think I would enjoy doing that"? On the other hand, maybe you have observed a parent, family member or friend on their job and it sparked your interest. This could be another way to assess your passion or skillset. Assessments can come from different sources. There are several online assessments out there, but sometimes you will come to this conclusion outside of an online test. Do not be afraid to receive the information from an informal source. Talk to people that truly know you. At times, it can be hard for you to look at yourself and pick out those qualities. Sometimes it takes someone telling you that you are an expert or that you are good at doing something before you actually realize it. Have you ever had people come to you for a specific reason? Then they start telling other people to go to you for that same reason. That may mean that you are good at whatever they are getting from you. Therefore, these messages can come from all places so be sure you are taking time to process all of them as potential career selections.

STEP 1 EXERCISE

1) Complete at least one assessment before moving on to the next step. If you don't have time to do it right now, make time over the next couple days. Set aside 30 minutes in the morning or before bed and get at least one assessment completed over the next 48 hours. It'll be helpful as you move on throughout the other steps.

2) Complete the following statements:
   a. My passion is

   _____

   b. My strongest skill is

   _____

   c. My talent is

   _____

STEP TWO
Shadow Day

When you're ready to purchase a vehicle, you will likely take it for a test drive, so you have a better understanding of what it is like to drive it. You may even research the make and model online before going to a dealership. Those are all very normal activities before purchasing a car. Think about when you're buying a brand new pair of shoes. How many do you try on before finding the perfect fit, color, style, and price? For myself, it takes at least 3 or 4 before I can find the right one. Either way, you should treat your career the same. The Shadow Day is the test drive of your career and a very important step. You may have to "test drive" a few different jobs before you find the right fit for you. There are no limits. If you're still feeling a bit uneasy after your second or third Shadow Day, continue looking for other options. Take your time and find the perfect fit. This is your career. This is how you will provide for yourself and your family so invest the time and take as many "test drives" as needed.

You've completed your assessment, but there are a few things to do before you get to your Shadow Day. First, start comparing your top selections. Read about those careers and see how and why people got started on that particular path. From there take your top selection list and start to dig in. What do I mean by digging in? Next to each job, list at least three different organizations/companies that offer that job/career. Then go to those specific websites and read about that organization. What are their values? What is their mission statement? Could you see yourself with this organization long-term? Look at their job descriptions to see if you are capable and have the ability to perform the job well. Once you have read up on those companies and figured out if they offer what you are looking for, now it's time to transition to shadowing.

Reach out to several companies and request a shadow day to see the "Day in the Life" of that job/position. The goal of Shadow Day is to gain enough information about that specific position or company to make a decision regarding your career selection.

"In my time recruiting for Early Talent and Interns, I found that it was very beneficial to allow shadowing sessions or side-by-sides with a more seasoned colleague. This allows for more realistic job preview in a more relaxed setting as opposed to classroom learning," said a ten-year Human Resource professional.

Sample Shadow Day Request Letter

Here is a sample letter requesting a shadow day from Dr. Randall S. Hansen, the founder of Quintessential Careers
https://www.livecareer.com/quintessential/sample-job-shadow-letter

Ms. Amanda Brown
JPMorgan Chase Bank
123 South Main Street #100
Colville, WA 12345

Dear Ms. Brown,

I am currently a student at Kettle Falls High School, and I am considering banking as a future career path. A family friend, Dr. Randall Hansen of Quintessential Careers, suggested that you might be willing to let me spend a day observing you so I can learn more about banking. I know I am asking quite a bit, but I would be extremely grateful if you allowed me to quietly observe you for a half- or full-day as you go about your usual schedule. If possible, it would be helpful if we also had a short interview toward the end of the shadowing so I could ask you any questions I might have about banking after observing your activities and actions. Thank you so much for considering my request. I will call you the week of October 10 to see about scheduling the job shadowing. If you need to reach me before that time, please feel free to contact me via phone (509-738-2922) or via email (xxxxxxx@yahoo.com).

Thank you for your time and consideration.

Sincerely,

Kylie Nelson

If you cannot find a contact from the website, utilize LinkedIn. This is also a good way to build your network within your desired industry. As you reach out to organizations, record the names and positions of each person you meet, and it is imperative to save their email address as well. Once you secure a shadow day, conduct more research on the company. Remember, this is for your benefit. You will get out of it what you put in it. Be sure to ask your contact person about expectations for that day.

Questions for the Shadow Day Contact

1) What is the dress code?
2) What is the visitor policy?
3) Is there paperwork I need to sign before arriving?
4) Will I shadow one person or multiple people?
5) How long should I prepare to be there?
6) What's the title and department of the Shadow person?
7) Cell phone policy

You want to be sure that you understand all of the expectations to avoid any surprises and to be sure you are making a good first impression.

39

Remember, you want them to know that you are interested in that career choice and that you are seriously considering their company for employment.

Next, you will need to create a list of questions for the person you'll be shadowing to be sure you can obtain the information needed to make a decision about that job and/or that particular company. Even if the person only has 30 minutes or an hour, you should still have a few questions or topics that you want to cover. Make sure your list has at least five questions but no more than 10 depending on how much time you will have with this person.

Sample Shadow Day Questions

1) What are your typical working hours?
2) How much of your work is individual work versus group work?
3) What type of skills are necessary in order to be successful in this position/company?
4) Is there anything I can be doing now that'll make me more equipped to be successful?
5) How has the economy affected this career?
6) Why did you select this company as your employer?

7) What is the difference between this company and the competitors?

8) Have you worked for any other employers?

9) How long have you been working here?

10) How did you get your current job?

11) How much of your day is spent behind the desk? Out in the field?

12) What are some of your biggest challenges you face in this job?

13) What is the most valuable lesson you have learned about this career, your job or life in general?

14) Do you expect the workplace to change much over the next five years?

15) What would you say are the biggest changes that have happened in this career field? Or will happen in the future?

The Shadow Day should be treated like it were an interview day. I would recommend you drive to the location the day before or the weekend before to avoid any issues getting lost the day of Shadow Day. You should arrive early so make sure you are planning enough time to account for traffic and other unforeseen situations. Do not forget to bring proper materials for note taking so you can capture everything. Please do not think you'll remember everything from the Shadow Day because this is all new to you and it is likely you will not remember half of it. Researchers have said after one hour people forget 50% of what they've learned, after a day 70% and after a week 90%. Notes will allow you to come back in two weeks and reference every topic from that day.

Once you arrive at Shadow Day, be sure you introduce yourself to everyone and let him or her know why you are there. "Hi, my name is _____, and I am here shadowing _____ in order to learn more about the position and the company overall." This introduction will give you even more exposure. You may only have the opportunity to shadow one person, but if you make an effort to introduce yourself to 10 other people, you have now created a larger network.

For example, I was working in my office one day and saw an unfamiliar face. About 5 minutes later, he was standing at my door with my co-worker. His name was James, and over the next 2 minutes, he introduced himself, told me why he was visiting and asked if I had a few minutes later on to chat. He wanted to know if I had any tips or suggestions on anything he should be doing in order to get a position on the team. Now, I was not the person he was there to see, but he leveraged that situation and created more contacts within his network by having his Shadow person take him around the workplace for introductions.

Now fast-forward six months later. James was interviewing for a position on our team. Of course, he had the upper hand because he knew most of the people in the office and over that 6 month period, he sent emails showing the work he was completing and explained how it related to the job he wanted. Therefore, the Shadow Day was very beneficial for him and helped him months later to secure a job on the team.

While you are shadowing a person and they are explaining their job, be sure you are taking notes. I've said this before and I will say it again and again and again. It is so imperative to take notes. I cannot stress that enough. Take notes about their primary job responsibilities as well as the special projects or the ad hoc tasks because you need to understand the things that you will do every day versus the things you will do every other week or once a month. Get clarity on words, acronyms, and processes that you do not understand. Sometimes the seasoned professionals have used words/acronyms so frequently and not realize it when sitting with you. So do not be afraid to stop them and ask for clarification. Be detailed in your notes, so you are able to make a decision once you leave about that position. The point is to be able to decide if this is something you really want to do every day. This is where your questions come into play. Make sure you are asking those questions you created before arriving. This is important because you want to be able to compare these same answers to other jobs that you may shadow in the future. If you run out of time, ask the person if you can contact them via email to ask the remaining questions.

Things to avoid on Shadow Day

Here are a few things I would avoid during Shadow Day. Do not ask about compensation. If someone begins to discuss compensation, do not respond or give your expectations. This is not the place or time to discuss compensation. Also, do not partake in a religious or political conversation. These topics are very personal for most people, and I would suggest staying away from them while in a professional environment. Even if there are people there that you know personally, you should still avoid these topics of conversation. Also, be sure to avoid asking personal questions related to kids, family, marital status or sexual orientation. Honestly, you should probably avoid these things during your interview period as well as once you get the job. The point here is to stay on task. Your job during the Shadow Day has everything to do with you getting your questions answered to see if this is something, you want to pursue as a career. The other topics are irrelevant and will get you off task.

After you have completed the Shadow Day, be sure to send Thank You notes. Hand-written notes are the most preferred because it gives that personal touch. I would suggest thanking them in person at the end of the day as well as sending an email or hand-written note. Be sure the note is intentional. Outline what you learned and how it relates to either your previous experience, your coursework or your desired career path. This is a way to show them that the Shadow Day was important to you and you valued the learnings. Also, include your next steps within the note. Let them know when you will be looking to start your career and ask for a future connection. This can be coffee, a quick phone call or a meeting in the office but be sure you try to set something up over the next 3-6 months to build upon the relationship you started during the Shadow Day.

Sample Thank You Note

Dear Mr. Smith,

Thank you for allowing me the opportunity to shadow your team for a few hours today. It was great to see your technology team in action. During my time with Ms. Tammy, I was able to see her present a new product to one of her customers via video conference. She was very knowledgeable about the product, and she knew exactly how the product would benefit her customer. I have been working within the technology world for two years, and I was excited to see Ms. Tammy reference software and programs that I have experience working with during my previous internships.

This opportunity was value-added and helped me to have a better understanding of the daily operation of your team. I am very interested in joining your organization and the Shadow Day simply reassured me that this is the right path for my career. I am graduating this Spring and will look to start my career over the Summer. I've been in contact with your HR manager, Sheila Davis, to stay up to date with new job postings. Is it okay if I send you an email or give you a quick call if I happen to have any further questions regarding your organization?

Thank you again for allowing me the opportunity to shadow your team today!

Sincerely,

Chris Brady

This is just a sample thank you note. The purpose is to be intentional about what you want and connect your skills to that particular job.

STEP 2 EXERCISE

1) Create a list of companies/positions to "test drive."

2) Draft a letter requesting a Shadow Day

STEP THREE
The Career Selection

A few years ago I met Mia and Alicia, two graduating seniors, at a career fair. They were close friends with the same major and happen to also be sorority sisters. Both were interested in pursuing a career within the banking industry. After spending 5 minutes with the two of them, I noticed Mia was passionate about the industry and had even completed an internship the summer before with J.P. Morgan Chase. Alicia said she was interested in the banking industry, but after speaking with her, I felt her passion was more focused on marketing. Like Mia, she completed an internship over the summer as well but with Macy's. I was stunned to see Alicia's face light up as she described her internship and how she had the opportunity to work on marketing campaigns. I could see in her eyes; she truly enjoyed this internship. I asked, "do you think you'll have this much excitement about the banking industry?" Immediately, her face dropped, and I could tell she really wanted to say yes, but she knew where I was going with my question. "I could do either!" she replied. I spent the next ten minutes talking about her passion and her skillset because she was right. She could definitely do either one, but which one would bring the most fulfillment? Which one would spark her interest and keep her motivated? The marketing internship with Macy's was her assessment and her test drive period. She was able to discover new skills and unveil a completely new passion. Today, Alicia is 5 years into building her marketing career and now holds the title of Brand Manager for a Fortune 500 organization. I am so glad she chose to follow her passion and not her best friend.

Career vs. Job

Did you know there is a difference between having a career and having a job? Anyone can have a job, but not everyone has a career. A job is something you do for an agreed upon price. A career is something you build in an effort to become the expert or professional within that field or industry. Do you see the difference? We all know people that get up and go to a job that they hate every day. Those people did not align their skillset with their passion or talent. They simply let the career choose them. Do not fall into that trap. Some people will say, "I just need a job. I don't care what it is." Unfortunately, that is the reality for too many people. They took a job not caring about the job description or the day-to-day responsibilities only caring about receiving a paycheck. In the beginning, it may seem fine and tolerable, but as time goes on, the stress, the misery, the unsatisfied feelings will all surface. Did you work hard in school to get a miserable job? I know you did not so take the time to find YOUR career.

Let's see how a career compares to a job. www.diffen.com has a comparison chart that helps with understanding the difference between the two.

Comparison Chart		
	Career	Job
What is it?	A career is the pursuit of a lifelong ambition or the general course of progression towards lifelong goals.	Job is an activity through which an individual can earn money. It is a regular activity in exchange of payment.
Requirements	Usually requires special learning that includes individualized components that develop abilities beyond that which training is capable of.	Education or Special training may or may not be required
Risk taking	A career may not mean stability of work as it encourages one to take risks. The risks are often internal and therefore planned.	A job is "safe", as stability of work and income is there. However shifting priorities, especially in resource jobs, can abruptly change the demand and require relocation which is an unstable factor. Risks may be completely external.
Time	Long term	Short term
Income	Varies depending on value to society or to some other entity. Non-monetary benefits may be higher. Salary is more common.	Varies by demand. More likely to be wage.
Contribution to society	May have high value as social change/progress may be possible.	May actually have a negative impact when counterproductive social practices are continued in the name of protecting jobs.

Hopefully, you have a better understanding of the differences after reviewing the comparison chart. As you go through this process, go back and reference this chart to be sure you're on the right track.

Now that you have completed your personal assessment and your shadow day, it is time to analyze your findings and figure out your career. This can be very easy for some of you and not so easy for others. It is so imperative that you take the time to evaluate your assessment and your shadow days to be sure you understand the best ways in which to align your passion with your opportunities and select the perfect career.

From your assessment, look at your top career choices and make a list of potential entry-level jobs within those careers. Once you have made that list, complete the following for each job title.

1) Visit the website
   a. Review their Values, Mission Statement, etc.
   b. Review job descriptions and determine the required skills and competencies
   c. Read the latest Press Release or News articles
   d. Review Quarterly Statements and performance success
2) Research their competitors and compare job descriptions

3) Utilize Glassdoor (or something similar) to get the inside scoop on companies with reviews from employees, salary tools, a plethora of their job postings and specific interview questions from current employees.

4) Search LinkedIn to see if you have connections to anyone working in those organizations and also to review profiles to gain a much better understanding of job descriptions.

5) Reach out to the human resource contact person and inquire about the employment process

   a. Find out how it works and what steps you will need to take to be considered for the next open position

Keeping track of all of this information is very crucial. Here is an example:

- Company Name: ABC Foods
- HR Contact Person: MJohns@abfoods.com
- Interested Job Title: Sales Trainee
- Typical Hiring Season: Spring and Fall
- Important Info:
  - Must apply by September 30th in the Fall and March 30th in the Spring

Try not to compare your assessment results with someone else's results because everyone is different. Just because you had the same major and took the same classes does not mean you should choose the same career. Mia and Alicia had the same major, but they are doing two very different jobs today. It's okay if your passion and interests are completely different. There are many students who end up interviewing with the same companies and taking the same interest in a company or industry as their classmates. This does not always have to be the case. You are doing yourself a disservice if you "follow the leader." Take charge of your future and make the best decision for your skillset and your passion. You select your career; do not let someone else have the control.

The career selection step is very important. It could be the difference between finding your perfect career now versus years down the road. As you narrow down the career list, dig deeper into the organization. Try to figure out how you will fit into that particular organization's culture. I know we have talked a lot about the assessment and the shadow day, but sometimes the deal breaker is the culture. How well will you operate in an environment that does not allow flexible working hours? Everyone must arrive at 8am and cannot leave until 5pm. Think about your learning style. How productive will you be in an "Open Office" environment? Yes, the office without any offices and everyone sits at a long table. Now some may have a partition between each person (sometimes called cubes) but most will likely not. Over the past few years, many organizations and companies have adopted this working environment. These are all things to consider as you select your career.

STEP 3 EXERCISE

Make your career selection by using both your assessment results and Shadow Day experience. List any companies that may fall under your career type.

Career	Company Name	Job/Position

STEP FOUR
Before the Interview

Michael Jordan is the greatest basketball player of all-time. In 15 seasons Michael gave the NBA a new meaning, brought new fans and exposure to other countries. He went on to win six NBA Championships and named Finals MVP in all six. The most impressive award is the NBA Most Valuable Player. Michael took it home 5 times.

During an interview with Ahmad Rashad, Michael Jordan described how he was pushed in practice to overcome defeat while playing a 5-on-5 game. Michael started out on Team 1, and the team led 5-2 half-way through the game. The coach stopped the game and switched Michael to Team 2. He knew what the coach was doing and just like that, Team 2 comes back and wins the game. "Those are all training tools for me and every day in practice was like that. So, when the game comes, it's nothing I haven't already practiced. I practice as if I'm playing in the game so when the moment comes in the game, it's not new to me. That's the reason why you practice.

So when you get to that moment, you don't have to think. Instinctively things happen."

What a compelling statement from Michael Jordan? "Instinctively, things happen." After you've practiced numerous times and reviewed the same materials, things will instinctively happen. This step is all about preparation and practicing for the interview.

Interviewing can bring on a mix of emotions. Most people are nervous because they want to perform well without making any mistakes. Some find interviewing to be difficult because of the unexpected questions. Others get really excited when it's time to interview because they consider it to be one step closer to their perfect career. No matter what type of emotions you have when you think about interviewing, this step will help you become more comfortable through preparation. Let's get started.

Now that you have all of your notes from each organization of interest, it is time to start applying for jobs and securing interviews. Most interviews are behavioral based so be sure to use the internet to find behavior based interview questions for the specific competencies from the job descriptions you listed in the last step. If the job description indicated the candidate should be goal-oriented, analytical and a team player, one should research those behavioral based questions. SEARCH: "what are some examples of goal oriented interview questions," etc. Make a list of those questions and start thinking about your best example for each question. Don't rush to answer each question. Simply read each question and write the first situation that comes to mind next to each question. After you've read at least 40 questions, start creating your list of examples based on what you wrote next to each question. There should be a few duplicate answers, but your list should be at least 15 examples after completing this exercise.

TIP: You should have at least 2 examples for each competency.

When your list is complete, it should look similar to the list below.
1.   Goal Oriented Example 1
2.   Goal Oriented Example 2
3.   Analytical Example 1
4.   Analytical Example 2

5. Team Player Example 1
6. Team Player Example 2

Sometimes you will be able to use one example for two different competencies. For example, a group project dealing with analysis could easily be used for team player and analytical. In a group, there are several ways to show how you were a team player and if the project dealt with data, you can use that to show your analytical work as well.

Based on your learnings from above, utilize the S.T.A.R. method to develop your examples. This technique is used to gather relevant information about a specific competency of the job. Your job is to tell a story within this format that will convey your ability to be successful in this role.

Situation. Task. Action. Result.

Situation – Before you jump into telling the actual situation, take the time to give the historical background. Give the interviewer the details behind the situation. Lay the foundation and then state your situation

Task – Give the interviewer your primary task and any specific details related to that task.

Action – Before you state behaviors, take the time to share your thought process. This is a good way to show the interviewer how you will process things on the job before taking action. Then state YOUR detailed behavior and be sure to focus on YOUR actions. This is key because you want the interviewer to easily identify your behaviors versus others.

Result – What happened? What did you learn from this example? Would you do anything differently? How does this example align with the competencies of the job?

Take time to develop quality S.T.A.R. examples. The key word here is quality, and that means powerful and memorable examples as well. Abraham Lincoln once said, "Give me eight hours to chop down a tree, and I will spend the first six sharpening the ax." You must spend the time developing these examples because this will set you apart from the other candidates. One recruiter told me "students are just not familiar with the interview process, nuances or best practices. They struggle with how to answer interview questions successfully while having a limited amount of professional experience to draw from." Use the S.T.A.R method, so you do not fall into this category. Write or type your examples because it will help to develop the most thorough answer possible. In order for it to be memorable, you must tell a story. The best way to tell a story is to have quality content and an impeccable structure or flow.

Sample Worksheet: Use this for each example

Situation

History/Background:

_____

_____

_____

_____

_____

Situation:

_____

_____

Task:

_____

_____

_____

_____

_____

Action:
Thought Process:

_____

_____

Detailed Behavior:

_____

_____

Thought Process:

_____

_____

Detailed Behavior:

_____

_____

Thought Process:

_____

_____

Detailed Behavior:

_____

_____

Result:

What Happened?

_____

_____

_____

What did you learn?

_____

_____

How does this behavior align with the competencies of the job?

_____

_____

Now that you have written out your examples, it is time to rehearse because words on a page means nothing if you cannot deliver. Take your time and go through each example. Think through all the details that are pertinent to making this a good example for the specific competency. Try not to overthink it. You're not writing a novel so leave out the "nice to know" details and focus on the "need to know" details.

Many people will suggest to always having an elevator pitch ready as well because you never know when you will have 30 seconds with someone to make an impression. Think about the three things you want someone to know about you if all else fails. That's your elevator pitch! It's short, simple and straight to the point.

Sample Elevator Pitch

Hello, my name is Ashley Jacobs, a graduating senior from Tampa, FL majoring in Accounting at the University of Florida. I am interested in pursuing an accounting career within the financial industry. During my college years, I was involved in several clubs and organizations including the Future Accountants of America. It was when I interned with Lincoln Financial and Ernst & Young that I discovered that I really enjoyed that field of work. Can you tell me about your Accounting department and structure?

Your pitch should be short but also informative. Start thinking of content for your elevator pitch because we will come back to it later on.

Self-Reflective Questions

The next phase of Step 4 is to develop answers to the anticipated self-reflective questions, which will typically ask for your opinion. They are usually asked at the beginning of the interview and helps to "break the ice" and relax the candidate. The interview will almost never be secured by nailing the answer to these questions, but it can surely be lost by not preparing for these types of questions. The key is to be intentional about the message you are sending through these answers.

Use the internet to research self-reflective interview questions. Here are a few examples:
1) Tell me about yourself?
2) Walk me through your resume.
3) What skills do you have that makes you a good candidate for this role?
4) Why did you choose our company?
5) Where do you see yourself in 5 years?
6) What is your leadership philosophy?
7) What is your greatest strength? Weakness?

A well-developed self-reflective answer should last less than one minute so do not overthink it. It may be helpful to create a few bullet points that you want to discuss and rehearse those points. When you are rehearsing, it should sound similar each time, and it's okay if a few words are different. The point is to get the content within each bullet point out there.

After preparing for your elevator pitch and self-reflective questions, you will need to focus on developing a close. Depending on the industry, this could be a very vital part of the interview. Many companies view a proper close as a sign of courage. A close does not have to be long. However, it should be memorable, and you should always start with a "thank you." Take your time and think about how you want to make your final impression on the interviewers and most importantly, find a professional way to "ASK" for the job. Here are a few examples:

"Thank you for your time and granting me the opportunity to interview. I'm excited about this position and hope you will consider bringing me onto your team."

71

"Thanks for taking the time to speak with me. Before I leave, I wanted you to know that I really want this job. My experience, as well as my education both, are perfectly aligned with your expectation."

"Thanks for having me in today. If you select me, you are guaranteed to get an energetic, dedicated and self-motivated person 100% of the time."

Those are just a few examples. You will need to craft a close that is authentic to you and the position.

Resume

At this point, you have prepared your self-reflective questions, your close and your examples for your behavioral based questions. Now it's time to prepare the resume. Recruiters and hiring managers want to see resumes that show relevant skills and how you applied them on the job, in the classroom or the community. Companies are only adding jobs to the payroll that will help them make money, save money or increase productivity. Every job added will bring value to the company one way or another. Companies receive hundreds of resume for each posting. One Human Resources Professional said she receives 200-300 for a 7 day posting. A Senior Director at Microsoft once told me "The purpose of a resume is to get an interview." The resume must grab the attention of the hiring manager or recruiter within a few seconds so you must do the work to make sure your resume has all the keywords pertaining to the job description, formatted neatly and filled with power action words leading each bullet point.

This is your opportunity to include any relevant experience. What if you don't have a lot of experience? That is okay. Think about the clubs or organizations you joined, participated in events or even held a leadership role. During that time, you may have helped the group solve a challenging problem. On the other hand, maybe you created a new process to help the team operate more efficiently. All of which are great experiences that should be included in your resume. Don't forget about the community involvement as well. Anytime you have the opportunity to work in a group or on a project to achieve a goal that would count as experiences and can be added to your resume. Never discount those because I know you learned something from each of them.

Take a look at these samples for structure and layout ideas. Your resume should be neat, easy to read and filled with keywords pertaining to the job description. It is very possible to be eliminated from the candidate pool if the recruiter has difficulty following your resume or cannot connect your experience with the open role. A corporate recruiter in the northwest region told me he looks at only 20% of resumes for each job posting. The first elimination tactic is the key word search. If the resume does not have the keywords, he immediately tosses it to the side. Think about this as you're modifying and updating your resume.

Ann Anderson
321 Spring St.
Charlotte, NC 28277
(555) 555-5005
AnnAnderson@xxxx.com

EDUCATION

University of North Carolina - Chapel Hill
Candidate for Business Administration May 2019
Concentration: Marketing 3.8 GPA
Dean's List: Spring 2017, Fall 2016, Spring 2016
Academic Scholarship Recipient

EXERIENCE

Macy's - Raleigh, NC   Sep 2015-Current
Sales Associate
- Training new hires on Macy's POS System, merchandising and product knowledge to ensure high performance
- Building a strong database of over 150 guest relationships to promote new merchandise and upcoming sales events
- Creating visual merchandising to support store merchandiser and increase sales
- Executing price changes, inventory control and marking items out of stock to guarantee customer satisfaction

Johnson & Johnson – Rogers, AR   May 2017-Aug 2017
Customer Development Intern
- Led analytics and developed strategies for NEUTROGENA Cosmetics and Bath brands at J&J Platinum customer ($64MM)
- Developed and implemented streamlined on-shelf availability monitoring process, reducing phantom inventory by $520k
- Directed qualitative market research for semi-exclusive Wal-Mart launch of Le Petit Marseillais developing national and retailer specific insights to support $6MM launch plan

AT&T Telecommunications – Chicago, IL   May 2016-Aug 2016
Business Sales Intern
- Increased customer leads by 5% leveraging SalesForce.com, enabling team to exceed quota
- Developed customized digital marketing campaign that reduced appointment lag time by 20%
- Refined sales reporting process that accelerated communication and reduced inefficiencies by 50%
- Placed Top 3 for National Intern Case Competition consisting of 75 interns across 15 teams

ORGANIZATION & HONORS
- Business Club - President **(2016 - current)**
- Volunteer, Central High School; tutoring and project planning **(2015-Present)**
- Winner of 3 Superior Lyceum Awards for Business **(2015-2017)**
- 2nd Place winner of the Lyceum of the Year Award **(2016)**
- Active member of a mentoring group, "Leaving our Legacy" **(2016-Present)**

SPECIAL SKILLS   Microsoft Excel: Expert, Microsoft Access: Intermediate, SQL Server, Data Analytics, Content Marketing, And Critical Thinking.

Ryan Washington

ryan.washington@ymail.com
Permanent Address: 5541 E. Beale Road, Dallas, TX 75216
mobile (469) 222-2222

EDUCATION:

Clark Atlanta University, Atlanta, GA - **May 2018**
Bachelor of Arts Degree in Mass Media Arts:
Concentration in Film - GPA: 3.59/4.00

EXPERIENCE:

FirstJob, Inc. - Atlanta, GA
February 2017 - Present
Brand Ambassador

- Enlisted 250 student signups through use of election campaign, guerrilla and social media marketing techniques in first 2 months
- Engage university students and professors in an energetic manner to provide knowledgeable information about the start-up company product offerings through use of 4 oral and visual presentations per semester
- Research events in the Atlanta University Center Consortium where target consumers are located to measure effectiveness
- Developed a competitor analysis to observe how competitors engage customers via social media and offered implementation suggestions

Clark Atlanta University; Office of Student Affairs - Atlanta, GA
May 2016 - August 2017
Orientation Guide

- Coordinated 7 academic workshops during Welcome Week and educated 800 prospective students on campus history, resources and student life
- Assisted Admission Counselors in maximizing their enrollment and campus guests by creating 2 promotional flyers and a video student testimonial
- Aided 45 first year students in the class registration process and development of class schedules

Clark Atlanta University; Athletics - Atlanta, GA
September 2015 - May 2016
Sports Information Director Intern

- Updated and maintained the official athletics web site by compiling statistics at athletic events
- Served as the liaison between the athletics department and 10 media outlets for 6 sports teams (Men and Women Basketball, Football, Softball, Baseball and Volleyball) for 120 student athletes
- Assisted in the production of 12 assorted athletic publications, schedule cards and posters

HONORS AND AWARDS:

Awards

August 2015 - *United Parcel Service Community Service Scholar, Scholarship Recipient,* $10,000

- Belief to accomplish the goal of academically uplifting the next generation of students through mentor-ship; 1 of 9 selected students

May 2015 - *Clark Atlanta University, Dean's List Scholarship,* $14,500

- Full-time student who has completed two semesters, achieved a minimum cumulative GPA of 3.30 and have no incomplete grades; 1 of 60 selected students

It's okay to have multiple resumes, as you should be modifying for each application. The modifications will increase your likelihood of getting a call back because you have aligned your resume so well with the position. If you are bold enough to list the company name within your objective, you better also be sure you double and triple check that resume before sending it to another company. A guaranteed way to be declined for a position is to list another company's name and/or position within your objective.

I'm sure your resume is committed to memory, but you should be ready to give a summary in less than two minutes of your experience and how it has positioned you to be a good fit for this role. It is very important to learn how to speak to your resume. Earlier we talked about preparing for the self-reflective questions, "walk me through your resume" and "tell me about yourself." These are very common self-reflective questions and you should anticipate getting them the majority of the time.

Asking Questions

"Students and new professionals are not sure of what questions to ask during an interview and as a result, tend to flounder and appear unprepared," said a professional recruiter in Charlotte, NC.

Interviewing is a two-way street so asking questions is imperative. You are interviewing the company just as much as the company is interviewing you. Typically, the interviewer will leave time towards the end for you to ask your questions. Therefore, it is wise for you to prepare those questions ahead of time. You want to ask questions that will reinforce your interest and passion for moving forward in the interview process.

Here are a few examples:

1) Can you tell me about the training I will undergo in the first 60 days?
2) How will I be evaluated in this position?
3) How is the team structured? How many people are on the team?
4) What is your management style? What are your expectations for this role?
5) When should I expect to hear back regarding your decision?

It is also a good idea to research the annual reports, any recent news articles and especially mergers and/or acquisitions. Be sure you are aware of all public information related to the company. These are all good topics for questions that will help you better understand that company.

Please do not ask about the following during the interview process:

1) Compensation – base pay, commission, 401k, etc. It is frowned upon to ask these questions during your interview time. If the interviewer shares any of this information, you should simply write it down but do not ask any further questions until you receive a written offer letter.

2) Do not request time off or ask about the vacation time allotted.

3) Do not request any special privileges at this time. If you need to arrive at 8:15am instead of 8am on Mondays and Thursday, this is not the time to make that request. Wait until you have an offer.

Rehearse, Rehearse, Rehearse

The last phase of preparation is the rehearsal stage. I cannot stress enough how important it is to rehearse before going to an interview. Remember, Michael Jordan said "instinctively, things happen" well that's how you want the interview to flow. Practicing will allow your instincts to drive the interview. You don't become an expert in interviewing in 24 hours. It is something you'll work on and build upon throughout your lifetime. No matter how great you feel about your examples, you can still fumble miserably if you do not rehearse.

> "Practice does not make perfect, it produces progress and consistency."
> – Unknown

I fumbled once and blew an opportunity that haunted me for a few years. It happened when I was a rising senior finishing up my internship with Ralston Purina. It was interview season, and I attended numerous corporate receptions on campus leading up to our career fair. I had my eye on a Sales Trainee position with Dell computers. I met one of the recruiters the year before and kept in contact. I nailed the first interview, and during the career fair, they gave me the good news. I was going to Austin, TX for the final round of interviews. It was such a phenomenal feeling. I remember sharing the exciting news with my Sales Management professor, Dr. Hightower, the next week in class. He was so happy for me and offered a few words of advice, "Do your homework, research the company, prepare your delivery and you'll be fine." I had all my examples written out, but I never rehearsed them. I didn't role-play with anyone and never actually spoke the words out loud. That was my mistake.

A week later as I was sitting in front of one of the Sr. Directors for Dell, I realized I was not prepared. I knew my examples, but I struggled with the flow of the details. I was all over the place, and the nerves didn't help. It was like being on stage addressing 500 people on a topic I knew like the back of my hand. But the shock of being up there, the lights, being the center of attention with every eye in the building focused on me and the words coming out of my mouth, felt like nothing less than my worst nightmare. I was so disappointed in myself. All the work I did last year by building the relationship with the recruiter, staying in contact with several of the employees, attending all of their events on campus – went down the drain. I still think about how bad I blew that one, but it motivated me to always prepare no matter the job. I don't ever want to experience anything like that again. Hopefully, you'll learn from my mistake and avoid this as well.

Find uninterrupted time in your schedule for this. You want to be comfortable with the ability to make mistakes. Try using a mirror, so you understand your facial expressions and body language. Reach out to a friend or a family member and ask them to role-play with you. This is an excellent way to get feedback from others as you are going through this process. Today, most people have smartphones that are capable of either video recording or voice recording. Either way, utilize these methods as tools while you are rehearsing your examples. It is very important for you to understand your facial impressions, your body language and the projection of your voice while going through your examples. These are things the interviewer will notice almost immediately but may be unknown to you.

For the record, a well-developed S.T.A.R. example should last at least 2 ½ minutes but take no longer than 5 minutes. If you are truly dedicated to developing your examples, it could take up to 45 minutes over multiple practice sessions to develop a well-rehearsed S.T.A.R. example.

In 2004 I worked for a wholesale plumbing company as a Branch Trainer and had an opportunity to create a training program for trainees. I didn't have much to start with, so I decided to develop a program that would benefit the organization as well as the individual. One trainee, Roger, graduated a few years prior. He previously worked for a small construction company before coming to us. I noticed during the interview process; he had trouble giving examples from his construction job. Roger listed several projects on his resume but couldn't quite communicate that during the interview. My boss hired him based on his experience, so I decided that I would help him improve his communication skills.

During his training, I specifically put him in situations where he would have to communicate a process or idea to multiple people. Roger struggled the first couple times, but during debrief, I could tell he really wanted to improve. He listened, took notes and practiced with me before presenting to the group. Each time was better than the previous, and he became more comfortable communicating his thoughts and ideas. By the end of the trainee program, Roger was comfortable enough to present a project to the entire office of 25 people. I was very proud of him because he stuck with it even through the times of discomfort and worked through it. My goal was always focused on the individual, and as I recruited and hired new trainees, I continued to create training plans to develop their biggest opportunity areas.

I have interviewed a number of people that were completely confident in their examples and delivery but bombed the interview because they did not rehearse. Do not let your ego get the best of you. Every person should rehearse before entering into an interview. No matter if the job is entry-level or for a Vice President position.

Preparation builds confidence and confidence is powerful.

"It's not the will to win that matters – everyone has that. It's the will to prepare to win that matters."
– Paul "Bear" Bryant

How do you rehearse for an interview without a script? You cannot so you have to write one. If you have followed the steps thus far, you have most of your script written already. If you have not, you have work to do. Go back and complete those steps so that you will have the pertinent information needed for your script. If you have researched and prepared carefully, you will have an idea of the type of questions you will be asked during the interview. Your preparation should bring you to a point where you are able to describe past positions, responsibilities, as well as your accomplishments.

Once you have the script written and you've rehearsed a few times alone, try role-playing with a friend or family member as I suggested before. Let them play the role of an interviewer so that you become more comfortable speaking about yourself in front of others. I would suggest using multiple people for different perspectives if you have the time. It is also a good idea to video or record yourself, so you are aware of facial expressions, pitch, and the inflections in your voice and your body language. All of these techniques will help you build the confidence needed to be fully prepared for your interview.

The final phase of the preparation is focused on positive visualization. Professional athletes, actors and yoga instructors do it all the time, and it works! In the days leading up to the interview, picture yourself sitting opposite the interviewer. Imagine yourself feeling relaxed, comfortable and at the top of your game. Play that clip over and over in your mind until it becomes so familiar, it actually becomes a part of your self-image. It simply cannot be stated too often, your confidence during an interview should be obvious and genuine.

Almost Show Time

As you get closer to the interview day, start gathering your materials to be sure you have everything you need. Start placing your 5-10 copies of your resume into your briefcase. If you don't have a briefcase, buy one or borrow one. Having a portfolio or a briefcase for your interview is important. This is essentially a component of your physical appearance and another opportunity for you to project that professional image you wear so well. You should also place a notepad and multiple pens inside your briefcase for note-taking purposes. A calculator is highly recommended and required for any job related to numbers. I would rather you have it and not need it versus not having it and needing it – you never know. If the company requested additional information such as transcripts, make sure you have copies of those handy as well.

The preparation phase is the most important part of the interview process so go back and re-read this information, so you do not miss anything.

At this point, you've done all you can do. You have spent time preparing and building your confidence so you can look the interviewer straight in the eye and deliver a phenomenal message. The night before the interview, make sure you get enough sleep. Try to go to bed early, have some warm milk, cocoa or herbal tea to relax your mind and body. Stay away from parties or anything that will keep you up late. Before going to bed, set your alarm so you can sleep comfortably. You are as prepared as you'll ever be.

Not every interview will be a success. You will not get the job every time but do not take it personally. It's not about you; it's about the needs of the company. However, you can increase the chances of success by presenting a professional, prepared and confident YOU to the interviewer. That is how you turn an interview into a job offer.

STEP 4 EXERCISE

1) Create or update your resume
2) Create a list of examples to be used during the interview.
3) Practice delivering your examples through the STAR method and role-play with a friend.
4) Develop the answers for the self-reflective questions and develop your close.
5) Develop your elevator pitch

It sounds like a lot of work, and it is but this is the time to invest in yourself. Break it up into segments but get it done.

STEP FIVE
During the Interview

The day of the interview you must be sure your attire is professional and acceptable. Rachel Zoe once said, "Style is the way to say who you are without having to speak." Your attire will speak professionalism as soon as you walk into the building when you are dressed for success! An interview is a performance with people playing different roles. Your role is the successful job prospect so play the part. Whether female or male, the conservative business suit is the recommended attire for any interview. If your business suit needs to be cleaned or pressed, send it to the dry cleaners. If you do not own a suit, buy one. It does not have to be a $1000 designer suit, but it should be a conservative navy blue, gray or black suit.

Business Professional vs. Business Casual

Attire is very important but it is also important to know the difference between business casual and business professional.

The business professional preferred attire for women is a nicely tailored skirt suit with a coordinated blazer, a well-pressed conservative blouse, flesh toned hosiery, and closed-toe low heeled leather shoes. Make sure the skirts are close to knee length. For men, a tailored suit with a conservative tie, clean, pressed dress shirt, and dark shoes. Make sure you are well groomed. Jewelry should be kept to a minimum. Ladies, something similar to a one-strand pearl necklace will suffice. Men, please remove all earrings, and no one should have any facial piercings.

Business casual is a more standard attire for the workforce and used by many organizations as a daily dress code. For men, a pair of khaki pants, button-down or polo shirt with loafers. For women, cotton dress, skirt, and blouse, or khaki pants and blouse. There are more options for women, but you also have to pay more attention to the fit, color, material, and style of your outfit. Also, keep in mind that if your outfit exposes cleavage, back, stomach or thighs, it is not appropriate.

Now you should have a better idea how your professional attire should look for the interview! It's time to leave for the interview. Be sure to double-check your briefcase to be sure you have all necessary materials. Look yourself over in a full-length mirror to be sure your attire screams professionalism. Leave your house in enough time to arrive 30 minutes early and do not forget to build in enough time to account for traffic and any other unforeseen issues. It may not be a bad idea to bring a bottle of water as well.

Based on all of your research and preparation, you should be able to generally anticipate how the interview will unfold. First, the exchange of genuine pleasantries, then the validating and self-reflective questions will likely follow. Next, the behavior questions focusing on the key skills and competencies that are needed to fill the role. Then it will be your turn to ask questions, and finally, you will close the interview!

If you have been following this guide, you are ready for this because you have been practicing. Now it is time to pitch your close! Smile, give energy and remember to thank them first. This is your chance to "ASK" for the job in a very professional way, so go for it! Remember it should not be long, but it should be memorable.

Tips for the interview

1) Do not read from your resume. You are talking about yourself and your experience – you got this! This is probably the best time to establish eye contact and exude confidence.
2) Be cognizant of your posture. Sit up straight with your feet flat on the floor.
3) Show a little personality throughout the interview but keep it professional.
4) If you bring your cell phone, turn it off or on silent.
5) Do not chew gum.

STEP 5 EXERCISE

Assess your wardrobe to ensure that you have professional attire ready and available.

STEP SIX
After the Interview

All of the heavy lifting is finally done! You should feel relieved that you made it through the interview. If you felt like it went really bad, do not worry or if you felt like it went really well, don't get too excited. Typically, interviews are not as bad as you thought but they're also not as good as you thought either. They usually land somewhere in the middle. If you felt like it was bad, it could be because you were overthinking it or you fumbled on a few things that you nailed during your practice time. All of those things are minor, and the best part is the interviewer usually has no idea when you fumble unless you make it known. If you felt it went really good, it's probably because you thought you nailed everything and that could be true, but there is always something that you likely missed. That too is minor and usually not a deal breaker.

At this point, there is nothing else you can do, except send a thank you note. Send it within 24 hours or on the same day. Make sure to review your strengths, skills, experience and why they should choose you for the position. Do not forget to list your contact information and thank them for the opportunity. If you do not get a response back after sending the thank you note, do not take it personal. Most interviewers don't respond back. A former corporate recruiter at Duke Energy told me that only a handful of interviewers respond to thank you notes – but they do expect to receive them from each and every candidate.

Let the waiting game begin! If you do not hear anything within the specified time given during the interview, it is recommended that you send a follow-up email. It should be very simple as you are only inquiring about an update. Most times, if you were not selected for the job, you will receive that information via email. If that is the case, do not be shy about sending a note requesting feedback for improvement. This is the perfect time to hear directly from the interviewing team and hopefully gain information that will help you during your next interview.

On the other hand, you receive a phone call from the hiring manager offering you the job! During the conversation, you will be ecstatic so grab a pen and paper and write down the important information.

1) Start date
2) Compensation – Salary, Bonus, 401k, etc.
3) Benefits – Medical, Dental, Vision, etc.
4) Background check instructions

If the offer is exactly what you wanted and you took the time to ask all the pertinent questions, accept it. If you like the offer, but you still have questions, ask for a 24-48 hour consideration period. During this time, do everything needed to figure out if the offer is a fit for you. Think about these things: Will the job require you to relocate? If so, is there a relocation package offered? How long will you have to wait for your benefits to kick in?

You are a superstar, and you impressed several companies, so you received multiple offers. That is the best position because you now have the power to choose which offer is a true fit for your passion and your talent, which will give you the highest form of satisfaction and fulfillment. This can also be an awkward time as well. For instance, if you receive an offer from Company A and you still have interviews to complete for Company B and C. This can be uncomfortable and a bit awkward if you do not handle them appropriately.

A 24-48 hour consideration period may not be long enough, but you should not reject a job with the hopes of landing another job. My suggestion is to be completely honest and let Company A know that you are still interviewing and would like an extension on your consideration period. Some companies will expect this with recent graduates, but it can also bruise the ego. Most companies will expect an immediate acceptance after making an offer.

This is an extremely exciting time! You are embarking on a new phase in life and starting to build your professional skills. As you start your new career, make sure you are prepared. From day one, your co-workers will start to build a perception of you. It is your job to be sure that perception is positive. For example, if your new career requires you to host clients over lunch or dinner, you should brush up on your dining etiquettes. Or if your new career requires you to drive daily, you should have a clean driving record. On the other hand, something as simple as a career that requires you to travel and you live alone with a pet, or you are a single parent. You will need to figure out a way to make this work. I know these examples sound so simple, but I have seen them happen several times. As you receive the offer, you are so excited and never think about these things until its week 1 or week 2, and you have an issue that will create a certain perception from your co-workers. Perceptions really are the reality no matter how well you explain your situation. Do not start your career trying to manage perceptions. Take care of those before Day 1 and ask the right questions before you accept the offer.

STEP 6 EXERCISE

Write down your perfect offer letter but be sure that it's realistic. This will help you understand if an offer is desirable enough to meet your expectations.

STEP SEVEN
The First 365 Days

You did it! You performed well in the interview and landed the job to start your new career! You asked all the right questions to be sure the offer was exactly what you wanted. Now, it's time to start your new gig and expand your knowledge and skill in this field.

Here are a few tips to help you get started in your new career:

Professionalism – be a professional at all times. You will always default back to this one. When in doubt, just be professional. What exactly does that mean? Let's break it down:

- Be on time. If your day starts at 8am, arrive at 7:30am. If it ends at 5pm, leave at 5:30pm. You are building a professional reputation and being punctual is an important piece of the puzzle. Arriving 10 minutes early is equivalent to being late. If they are serving breakfast before the meeting, arrive early enough to eat breakfast, use the restroom and be in your seat 10 minutes before the start time. Do not eat during the meeting especially if time was allotted prior.

- <u>Use good judgment with dress codes especially the ladies.</u> "Casual Friday" is not your opportunity to show off your most stylish or less than stylish attire. Do not wear jeans with holes in them. I know they're super stylish and cute, but they are not professional. Some of you may take it the other way by wearing old t-shirts, dirty shoes and even hats. Stay away from all of these things. Dress code is important and if there's any doubt, don't wear it. Ladies should abide by the two inches above the knee rule (or fingertip rule), and the "touch your toes" test. Use a floor length mirror while getting dressed. Once you're done, turn your back to the mirror and touch your toes. If anything looks or feelings uncomfortable, don't wear it. Also, ladies do not wear the low cut shirts. If that's all you have, go out and buy more or wear a camisole underneath.

- <u>If you are friends with co-workers, be sure your actions are still professional with them</u>

<u>in the workplace.</u> To be on the safe side and limit your personal conversations with them – avoid discussing weekend plans or previous events especially if those events are inappropriate for the workplace.

Email Etiquette – be careful because email will more than likely be the primary form of communication. Your emails should be detailed but concise. Don't write a book but give enough information, so the message is received and understood by the recipients.

- ALL CAPITAL LETTERS typically means you're yelling at your audience or being lazy.
- I think the worst email offense is hitting the "reply all" button for something only the sender needed to know. Or being the person that hits "reply all" and says "please do not hit reply all when responding." Those people are comical. Either way, don't use reply all unless your message is pertinent for the entire group.
- When you are typing an important email, be sure to insert the receiver's name(s) at the very end. You want to avoid accidentally

sending it too early or the receiver seeing an incomplete thought.

- If you receive an email that causes conflict or poses disagreement, think through your response before hitting the "send" button. The unfortunate part about emails is – you can't take them back. Once it's out there, it's out there. So, think about it long and hard before throwing something out there. Also, don't be afraid to respond the next day either. Sometimes that is the best path.

Alignment – make sure you understand how you will be measured, how your boss is measured and how your overall team will be measured. You must align your goals to support the success of your team and your boss.

Network – Set up 15 minute 1-on-1 introduction meetings with your team members to help you understand how each person contributes to the common goal. Invite them to coffee or lunch to get away from the office but make sure you understand their contribution and the level of interaction you will have with each of them.

Curiosity – Ask "Why"! As the new face in the office, you have the autonomy to question every process, structure, idea, etc. Asking why something is the way it is, forces people to think about the "why" behind their actions. This isn't a bad thing if executed in a genuine way. The reason companies hire new people are to fill open roles and gain a new perspective that'll hopefully drive success for the organization. Remember, you're the fresh eyes on the business so don't be afraid to share what you see versus what they have seen for years.

Take Notes – This is very important. There's nothing worse than spending time with a new hire and reviewing several things, and two weeks later we're having the same conversation. This is a waste of time and disrespectful. I don't care if you use a program like One Note or if you whip out a pen and paper. Either way, take notes so you can refer back to them at a later date. Some things may not make sense, or you may have a hard time understanding what's going on, however, continue to jot down the notes, and eventually, it'll all come together

Understand the "Big Picture" – You are directly connected to your individual goals, team goals and department/division goals but don't forget about the company goals, mission, strategy, and vision. The executive leaders within the organization are all focused on the "Big Picture," and you should find a way to tie your work to the "Big Picture."

Integrity – do what you say you're going to do. Follow-up and ask questions if needed. If you are unable to meet the deadlines and expectations, be sure to communicate this and provide an update on how you will meet the deadline or expectation.

Be an Expert – do everything you can to be the expert in your area. Become a sponge and absorb as much information as you can about the company, your department and your team. There's no better feeling than being the new person on the team and able to answer pertinent questions related to your team or department.

The first few weeks or even months will be overwhelming. Stay focused and communicate early and often, especially when you do not understand or are possibly confused about something. Taking the initiative and always being proactive are two key traits to master early in your career. Play to your strengths and develop a plan to address your areas of opportunity. Pay close attention to what takes you off task and/or what activities that keep you from being your very best. Make sure you reach out to people who can help you get through those critical times because EVERYONE has or will go through tough times in life and throughout their career. Remember, we were not created as islands unto ourselves, and you are not expected to build on your own. Don't isolate yourself. At times the best learnings will come through collaboration with others. At the end of the day, study your craft and always put your best foot forward.

DINING ETIQUETTE

Most people are familiar with the basic dining etiquettes such as not speaking when your mouth is full, not telling inappropriate jokes or covering your mouth when you cough. Those are easy. In fact, most children understand those guidelines. What about the other etiquettes that aren't as familiar? Have you ever taken a sip from the wrong water glass? That can be kind of awkward. What about trying to figure out the perfect bottle of wine for the table? The one that gets me almost every time is the napkin. While eating it's in my lap but what should I do with it when I stand to go to the restroom? Etiquette is important, and if you've selected a career that requires business dinners and/or customer entertainment, you may want to brush up on your dining etiquette knowledge.

Here are a few tips I have shared with several students over the past few years.

1) Your attire is very important. If you are dining at a high-end restaurant, you should wear a suit. Men should wear a jacket and tie

and ladies should wear a jacket with pants or a dress suit.

2) Introduce yourself to everyone at the table and try to engage in conversation with all of them.

3) Sit up straight with your feet flat on the floor. If you must cross your legs, only do so at the ankle. Also, do not take your shoes off.

4) Don't put your cell phone keys or purse on the table. It's a huge distraction and suggests that you aren't fully engaged with the table.

5) Leave your pet peeves about restaurants at home. This means do not ask for a glass of hot water to clean your utensils before using them. That is considered a direct insult to the restaurant.

6) Do not take pictures of your food. This has become popular, but it is inappropriate for professional dining. Do this on your own personal time.

7) When the host unfolds her napkin, this is your signal that the meal has officially started. You can then unfold your napkin. The napkin remains on your lap throughout the entire meal and should be used to gently blot your mouth.

8) You can start eating when your host starts eating. As the waiters start to bring food to the table and not everyone has food yet, don't begin to eat. The polite gesture is to wait until everyone has been served the first course, and then begin to eat together. Sometimes the host may encourage you to "Go ahead, please don't wait." In this case, it's okay to start eating.

9) Use the utensils farthest from the plate, working from the outside in.

10) Your liquids are on the right, and your solids are on the left. If you make a circle with your index finger and thumb (straighten the other three fingers), you'll see a "b" on the left hand and a "d" on the right hand. That is an easy way to remember your "d" or drink is on the right, and your "b" or bread is on the left.

11) If you must leave the table during a meal for any reason, do so with as little disruption to others as possible. Politely and quietly excuse yourself and lay your napkin on your chair.

12) Do not cut your food into small bites all at once. Only cut two or three bites at a time and once you've eaten those bites, cut another two or three bites.

13) When you're not eating, keep your hands on your lap or with wrists resting on the edge of the table. Elbows on the table are acceptable only at the end of the meal when no food is on the table.

14) The host signals the end of the meal by placing his napkin on the table. You should follow suit by placing your napkin neatly on the table to the left of your dinner plate, with no soiled areas showing. Don't place your napkin on your plate or try to refold it.

TESTIMONIALS

"Latoya has played a vital role as a mentor in my career. Specifically, as I transitioned from being an undergraduate student into a young professional at a Fortune 100 company. As a mentor, Latoya has enhanced my personal and professional development through helping me understand the business environment, identifying ways that I can bring value to my team, and most importantly, helping me identify my leadership capability. Having the opportunity to be coached by such a seasoned and successful professional also shorten my learning curve, enhanced my productivity in the workplace, and helped me better align with my teams business strategy. Although Latoya has equipped me with a plethora of skillsets, the one I appreciated the most is the time she spent on her weekends to ensure I was prepared for my interview. Latoya, shared several tools to assist me in my interview preparation which set the stage for my career. These tools included a PowerPoint presentation that outlined the STAR method, interview prep worksheets, and we even practiced over the phone. As a mentee, having Latoya as my mentor means so much to me because I am the first in my family to work for a Fortune 100 Company and her guidance has helped me start a foundation for generations to come." - Dominique Golden

"Senior year of college is one of the most challenging parts of your college experience. The feeling compares to the overwhelming anxiety of receiving your acceptance letter, except this petrifying terror is from the unknown. I constantly remember asking myself, what's next? The answer was always very vague, or unclear. My moment of realization came when I was sitting in my Business Marketing class and a recruiting team from Nestle came to speak with us. After their presentation they left most of my peers filled with curiosity, but for me it answered the burning question I had lingering in my head for months. I will never forget the eye opening advice shared by one of the presenters Latoya Pearson, she said " Every interview you go into you should be answering with the STAR method, providing what the situation is, what tactic you used, the action your took, and the result." - Jhonae Mozeke

"Practice, practice, and of course –practice! Latoya was so kind and patient with me. She instilled not only the importance of practice but how to properly practice in a way that would guarantee me a successful interview. I'm a well developed interviewee thanks to her." – Destiny Smith

"Latoya has always been willing to develop the members of her team, and offering to help with my interview process was no different. The most beneficial piece for me was performing a mock interview with her. It provided me with the opportunity to hear honest feedback from someone who had seen my strengths and weaknesses day in and day out in my current role. Her manner of breaking down the question and helping you identify the true meaning behind it is unmatched." – Emma Brock

REFERENCES

1) Norris Wright, MBA – Sales Professional

2) Candice McPhatter, MBA – Human Resource Professional

3) Erica Nicholson – Human Resource Professional

4) Briana Orsborn, Student

5) Jalon McGhee, Student

6) Holland Code
   https://www.123test.com/career-test/

7) MAPP Assessment
   www.assessment.com

8) Aptitude Test
   www.oprah.com/omagazine/Aptitude-Tests-Career-Assessment

9) Career Quiz
   https://www.princetonreview.com/quiz/career-quiz

10) https://www.washingtonpost.com/news/grade-point/wp/2015/01/30/more-

than-4-out-of-5-students-graduate-without-a-job-how-could-colleges-change-that/

11) http://www.reuters.com/article/usa-studentloans-jobs-idUSL2N0KG1SW20140106

12) http://usatoday30.usatoday.com/money/economy/employment/2010-05-19-jobs19_CV_N.htm

13) http://www.acenet.edu/newsroom/Pages/Demographics-of-College-Graduates.aspx

ABOUT THE AUTHOR

Latoya is a Retail Team Leader for Nestlé Purina Petcare. In her position she is responsible for driving business, people and organization development across the East region for the Pet Specialty Retail Team. A native of Gainesville, Florida, Latoya attended Gainesville High School and earned a scholarship to Florida Agricultural & Mechanical University, where she earned her Bachelor of Science degree in Business Administration.

Upon completing her undergraduate degree, Latoya began her career as a Sales trainee for Ferguson Enterprise. She served several roles with increasing responsibility across a variety areas. During this time, she earned an MBA with a concentration in HR Management from the University of Phoenix. Following her passion for sales, Latoya joined Nestlé USA in 2006 as a Retail Sales Representative. In 2008, she was accepted into the Sales Development Program which is a leadership program for high performing sales representatives. Latoya was promoted to Sales Analyst in 2010 and supported several customer teams within the grocery and mass channel. In 2013, Latoya was promoted to the 4th highest Account Manager position within the organization. She managed nearly $300 million for the Walmart Cat Litter business before moving into her current role.

In 2009, Latoya took the Co-Lead position for the recruiting team at the Atlanta University Consortium (Spelman, Morehouse and Clark Atlanta). Her leadership has resulted in successful recruiting, hiring and promotion of several AUC graduates. Latoya conducts interview workshops, mock interviews and professional development workshops with students each semester across several campuses. She also mentors students as they're transitioning into their career.

Latoya is a member of the Queen City Metro Chapter of 100 Black Women where she serves on the Boad of Directors and as Chair of the Communications & Nominating committees. Latoya served as a foster parent for 2 years and has continued to work with the foster care community on several projects and programs. She maintains a relationship with all of her previous foster kids and still spends time with them.

Latoya loves to travel, read, write poetry and relax on the beach. She has lived in 6 different states since graduating from college and currently resides in Charlotte, NC. Latoya has 3 siblings and 4 nephews that she loves to spoil.

Made in the USA
Columbia, SC
05 October 2017